Destroy Nerves and Pass Your Driving Test

Simon Capon

Table of Contents

An Introduction: 1

You Have What It Takes 2

It's Not About the Result 6

Your Mission 8

Your State of Mind 10

How Do I Look? (Physiology) 11

Why Do I Get So Nervous? 16

A New Way of Thinking 19

Words Are Powerful 23

The World of Visualisation 33

A Virtual Experience 35

You Can Do Anything (Beliefs) 39

The Hidden Gems 50

Attitude and Focus 53

Summary 57

An Introduction:

Simon Capon is a trainer and master practitioner in the psychology field of Neuro-linguistic programming (NLP) and recognised by the 'The Association for Integrated Psychology' (AIP). During the last fifteen years he has brought together a collection of psychological skills and techniques to create a system called, "It's Time to Start Winning." As a result of this system he has worked with GB Athletes, Para-Athletes, Professional footballers, golfers, tennis players and five world champions. He has written for Tennis Life and Golf Punk magazines and is currently a columnist for UK Tennis magazine. Simon has also appeared in the BBC documentary *Race for Rio*.

You Have What It Takes

"What we want the most are generally things we have to work the hardest for." I remember this being said to me the afternoon I failed my first driving test. The instructor drove me home with an uneasy silence which was finally broken as he attempted to lighten the mood. As the car pulled up outside my home, I noticed the front door opening and my mum appeared with a look of hope which changed dramatically as my expression said it all. My instructor did his very best to console me, "it's just the nerves getting the better of you," he explained, as he opened his diary ready to book further lessons. This was nothing short of devastating. I made my way into the house and contemplated what had just happened. The instructor pointed out that he was as stunned as I was, "you are certainly good enough to pass," he said thoughtfully. So, what happened? Why and how did it all go wrong?

Fast forward thirty years and I now spend a great deal of time working with sports women, men and teams creating the ultimate mindset. Students range from fun runners to world champions. No matter what their level of ability, all want to achieve an ambition that will stretch them both mentally and physically. Regardless of what sport is played, it's generally accepted that you first find a coach to work with who is qualified to teach the skills required. You practise and rehearse until you reach a level where you can realistically accomplish the outcome or goal that you have set. The biggest challenge is to bring all you have learnt to a one-chance-only opportunity.

If you are competing for a club title or a world final, you must be at your best when the match commences, or the starter gun fires. No one is going to wait for you, it's entirely your responsibility to turn up with a clear mindset that is focused with confidence and the certainty that you will produce a performance of the highest standard when you need to the most. This is evident when the sporting elite show incredible confidence and clarity of thought during their biggest events. The ability to remain calm and confident when the pressure is at unimaginable levels is a behaviour that *can* be learnt. It's easy to come to the conclusion that it's their genetics and that some have natural ability whilst most don't. However, it's vital to recognise that this is nothing other than a set of skills that anyone can acquire and master.

After a training session with an athlete preparing for the World Athletics Championship, I was asked by a friend to speak to his cousin who was incredibly anxious regarding his upcoming driving test. He had failed his test twice although his instructor was firm in his belief that he was an excellent driver, but during his test he simply fell apart. His mind hit the panic button and he became a fraction of the driver he demonstrated during lessons. As we began our work together it became clear that I was simply coaching him with the same set of skills that I teach the athletes. He was working on all the same techniques, but instead of using them for a sporting scenario he would implement them to pass his driving test. Up until this point when it came to the test, he simply didn't have the psychological tools to duplicate his level of driving during lessons to the same level when taking his test. He was technically good enough but arrived for his test with nothing more than hope that he would feel confident and focused. He assumed he lacked the elusive bottle (nerves of steel) that was required to remain confident during a pressurised situation. The reality is that everyone has these reserves of courage; they just need to know how to access them. I gave him a new set of skills which he practised with the same enthusiasm he demonstrated during his driving lessons. He passed his test at the next attempt which left me with a thought, how many people fail their test simply because their anxiety becomes so strong that their confidence dissolves and their self-belief departs? I began working with more people, of all ages, some taking their test for the first time and others who had failed multiple times. Yet all without exception were arriving at the test centre with little or no plan on how they would control their mindset and emotions.

Obviously, I'm only able to work with a fraction of the people who are suffering with nerves and anxiety as they count the days leading to their test, so I made the decision to write down the formula I use, for everyone to learn. Of course, nerves don't simply arise on the day of the test, you are likely to experience unwanted emotions weeks before. So, much of the system is based on changing the data that is stored deep in your unconscious mind. Essentially you rehearse the skills and become more competent. In time you automatically react to pressurised situations very differently and ignite the emotions that work for you. If you are easily put off by overcomplicated data and instructions, then this book is most certainly written for you. This is not an instruction manual for the mind, but is a guide to learning a few simple techniques that will give you the tools you need to dramatically change your emotions from severe anxiety to excitement. You will be in control of your actions and emotions, increasing your chances of a successful driving test. During this book I will explain why this happens and share with you some game-changing techniques, some of which will require time investment whilst others will have an instant impact. You will learn how to produce confidence with a different posture, reprogram the data that creates your reality and generate emotions that work for you and not against you. I'll introduce you to your new best friend and coach, as well as teach you a skill that takes you from high levels of anxiety to excitement in just a few seconds. Couple these skills with other components of the system and you will not only become a more confident and self-assured individual, but will be totally prepared to take your test. When you know how to produce confidence and self-belief, your whole perception of taking your test will change significantly. Take a moment to imagine how life will be when you have your full license. You can forget having to rely on lifts from friends and family, or waiting for the bus in the rain, and begin to enjoy your new freedom. Remember your instructor knows you are ready for your test so all you need is a new mindset, and life will change dramatically. So, let's begin.

It's Not About the Result

The sole reason you are reading this book is to pass your test. In other words, your focus is on a result. It's certainty important to know exactly what you want. However, when you place your attention entirely on the result you will almost certainly consider the possibility of failure. I'm sure you have experienced anxiety in the past when you were taking on a task that was going to be extremely challenging. Without any conscious thought your mind shifted and you contemplated the prospect of disappointment. As you will discover shortly, we are all pre-programed to avoid failure, so to begin with I will guide your thinking in a new direction. Let me introduce you to the cycle for success.

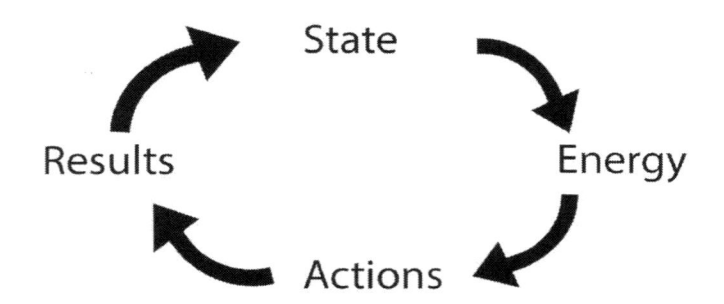

State → Energy → Actions → Results → State

Let's assume it's the morning of your test. You are sat in the driving seat and the examiner is sat with you. You are suffering a state of fear and apprehension. I'm sure in the past you have experienced this uncomfortable state and felt any positive energy drain away. This of course has an immediate impact on your actions, and your ability to drive at the level required has all but vanished. This leads to a disappointing result and you fail your test, which reinforces your fragile state that driving tests are nerve-racking and incredibly uncomfortable.

Let's look at a very different scenario. You arrive at the test centre with a state of excitement, focus and clarity. You feel the levels of energy in your mind and body building. The test begins and your focus and clarity of thought allow you to place all your attention on the job in hand. Your ability to drive at your usual level produces the desired result and you pass your test. At this stage you may conclude that you have four components to pay attention to, but the reality is that you only need two. If you focus on your state (which is what you will learn in this book) and the actions (what you learn from your instructor), your energy and (most importantly) the result will take care of themselves. I can almost hear people saying, "that's easier said than done." The answer is yes, at this point it certainly is, however you will learn how to create this state when you need it the most. It will take commitment, but everything you now find easy was at one time difficult. You didn't sit in the driving seat for the first time and expect to be test ready the same day. The things we want the most require a price; it's not always a financial one, and this one requires your time. Make a promise to yourself that you will read, practise and go for it! Just like the athlete, footballer or golfer who know their outcome and direct their attention to learning the skills required that will help make their dream a reality.

- **Focus on your state & actions.**
- **Be patient**

Your Mission

I'm sure you have been told to have goals in your life, and a well thought plan. As the saying goes "when you fail to plan, you plan to fail." This is crucial unfortunately; the word *plan* doesn't really produce much excitement. Likewise, goal is overused, and its impact has diminished significantly over time. Although these terms lack power, their purpose is important so you need new headings and categories that produce more energy and a greater impact. Take a piece of paper and divide it into three columns. At the top of the first column label it '**The Mission**.' This is your goal, which is of course to pass your driving test. In the second column write at the top '**Mission Statement**.' These are the tasks and details you must implement to pass your test. Tasks can be booking lessons, allocating time in your diary, ensuring your time with the instructor is productive, and allowing enough time to arrive early for the lesson, with adequate traveling time for your next engagement. The details are your knowledge of the highway code, your ability to drive to the standard required, and your competence to produce a mindset of focus, clarity and confidence. When you master all the components in your mission statement you will arrive at the test centre with all the confidence and certainty you will need to execute a driving performance to the very best of your ability. Finally, column three is labelled '**Purpose**.' Whenever you are facing a task that will take you away from your comfort zone it's important to have motives that are so powerful that any time your enthusiasm begins to decline you can instantly refocus and get back on track. We all have a different purpose, however yours may be to enjoy more freedom. No more asking parents, family or friends for lifts or waiting at the bus stop. Perhaps you need a full license for a better career, or you may be a busy parent. Having your own car will make life for you and your family considerably easier. Take some time over this and include all the motives you can think of. At this point you may be thinking, just a few paragraphs ago you said I should place all my attention on the performance and not the result. This is still the case, but you must first have an outcome (Mission) before undertaking any tasks. Having an agenda (Mission Statement) that will guide you is vital and during those difficult times when the enthusiasm dwindles having a clear purpose that will relight your fire will be essential. I would normally recommend that you look at your mission every few days, however it's likely that your test will be at the forefront of your mind, so you won't need any reminding. However, taking a look at your mission statement should be a daily occurrence knowing that your purpose is there if you need a burst of encouragement. To clarify, you know your mission (to pass your driving test) and your mission statement (your tasks and details), so focus on these every day. Remind yourself of your purpose whenever you need to reignite your desire, then place your entire attention on your state and performance.

- *The Mission* **is your goal.**
- *The Mission* **Statement includes the tasks & details.**
- *Purpose* **is a list of motives.**

Your State of Mind

As you have already discovered, your state or state of mind is going to be vital. The big question is, what is it and how can you create one that will lead you to a driving test where you are confident and certain that you have a set of strategies in your locker that you can deploy whenever required? State is simply how you feel about yourself and your ability to take on any challenge you face. When you are in a state of uncertainty you can lose control of your thinking and fear can strike at alarming levels. This is extremely uncomfortable and for some people it's completely terrifying. When experiencing a state of confidence, you feel alive and even unstoppable. It's as if you are two different people but the only component that has changed is the state you experience. This is important to grasp as it places you in a very powerful position. You can design and produce any state you wish; you must first look at how you can consciously manufacture a desirable state. Your state is made up of two components. They are physiology, how you position your body as you stand, walk or sit, even the way you smile in fact anything you do physically. The second component is internal representation which is simply the thoughts you have in your mind.

- **Your state is how you feel about yourself and your ability to take on a task.**

How Do I Look? (Physiology)

Have you noticed someone walking past you whom you have never met or even seen before, yet you instantly know they are extremely confident with a strong self-belief? It's highly likely that you were very accurate in your assumption, but how is this possible without any form of verbal communication? When you take on a physiology that you associate with confidence, it automatically encourages a state that is in line with it. Take yourself back to a specific time you felt certain regarding your ability to perform a task or an outcome you set yourself. Recall the way you held your posture, the pattern of your breathing and even the tone of your voice. Now take yourself to a different time. This one is during a situation when you felt anxious or apprehensive. Again, pay attention to the way you positioned your body, your breathing and your tone of voice. It will be significantly different to the one you experienced when you felt confident. Just for fun sit down and lean forward, bow your head and say in a tone of hesitancy "I feel amazing, nothing will stop me from being extraordinary and full of energy." Firstly, notice how difficult that is. You probably find it difficult to even remain in that position. Most will conclude they produce a physiology of confidence when they are feeling confident, but as you know if you take on a strong physiology your mind will create a state that mirrors your posture.

Whilst training many years ago I attended a seminar with a small group in Scotland. We were told that the speaker for the morning session had travelled in from the USA. I sat next to a lady who shared my enthusiasm and we waited patiently for his arrival. The speaker then walked across the stage, put his hand up and said "Good morning!" He then continued walking and made conversation with one of the event organisers. The lady sitting next to me turned to face me, smiled and said "Now there's a confident man." I agreed and then asked, "How do you know he is confident?" She looked puzzled and declared, "I don't know, but I'm sure he is." Five years later I was asked to speak at an event and I discovered the American speaker was also attending. This was the perfect opportunity to thank him for his talk five years ago. It was an extremely busy event but I finally caught up with him and asked if he remembered the event in Scotland five years previous. He looked to the sky and said, "I remember it very well; I was having an extremely challenging day. The airline had unfortunately mislaid my luggage and the hotel had double booked my room. So, I now had no clothes and no accommodation. But the show must go on!" I smiled and replied, "But you seemed so confident?" He smiled and answered, "Well of course, I'm always confident." I paused then probed deeper. "So how do you create so much confidence?" He then shared with me his secret. "It's all in my physiology. Before I step out on stage, I spend a few seconds creating a simple breathing pattern. It can be any pattern you wish as long as there is a rhythm. My rhythm is breath in through my nose for 5 seconds and exhale through my nose for 6 seconds. It makes no difference what the rhythm is as long as it's consistent. I then check my posture and make the alterations if required. I stand tall proud with my shoulders back, head held high and chest out. If it's appropriate I may say out loud "come on!" If not, then I give myself the same command but with my internal voice. I then ensure every step I take and every gesture I make is one of complete certainty. When I walk into a room I don't wave at the audience, I put my hand up and say with authority "good morning!" To me this was pure gold from a world-class speaker. He had taken an idea and packaged it so anyone could master it. Whenever I work with a sports or non-sport client, the first exercise is to correct their physiology.

To help achieve this, follow this exercise:

1. Stand up tall with your head held high, chest out, shoulders back, and smile. Exaggerate this so you feel you are overdoing it. It's unlikely you generally adopt this position, so it will feel slightly strange unless of course you are at this moment feeling very confident.

2. Place your hands on your hips (it's ok we won't start any dance routine).

3. Pay attention to your breathing. When people are stressed, they tend to breath high up in the chest. Breath from the stomach, this area is where your calming receptors are located. It may be difficult in the early stages to breath from the stomach so place one hand on your stomach and one on your chest. Focus all your attention to your stomach and feel it inflate like a balloon as you inhale and shrink as you exhale.

Within a short space of time this will become second nature.

4. Create a rhythmic, smooth breathing pattern by inhaling and exhaling through your nose. Take some time to produce a pattern that is comfortable for you. Pay attention to your posture, make sure you remain in this strong position throughout the exercise.

5. Continue this for two to three minutes.

6. You will begin to notice a change in your state. If you were feeling any anxiety a few minutes ago, you are now experiencing a transformation where the anxiety levels are replaced with a more controlled confident state. If not, then exaggerate the posture a little more and breathe deeper.

7. To finish the exercise (if it's appropriate to do so) shout or say loudly "Come on!!"

In just a couple of minutes you have changed your biochemistry. The only alteration you made was your physiology, and you didn't need any change in your environment or what was happening around you. Most people have a belief that their environment or circumstances need to change in order for their emotional state to alter. They believe they must have a reason to feel confident, excited or happy. The reality is, that any state is within your control and it begins with a few simple adjustments to the way you stand, move, breath and use your voice. Physiology is the fastest and easiest way to make the transformation. You can make the appropriate amendments and it takes seconds. The second component will take more effort, but the benefits are life changing.

- **The way you position your body has a direct effect on your state.**

But first let's answer the most important question of all.

Why Do I Get So Nervous?

We are all equipped with the most remarkable piece of biological engineering known to mankind and it's called the human brain. It has evolved considerably, however there is one part that is still primitive in the way it operates and is responsible for our emotions. To simplify things, we will refer to it as the "emotional brain". Your emotional brain is designed to keep you safe and alive. It achieves this with three prime directives. Firstly, our **fight or flight response**. During a primitive time when we came face to face with a predator, our mind would use energy from other parts of our bodies and distribute it to our limbs and upper body so we could fight or run for our lives. This was once frequently required; however, we now live in a more comfortable environment. The importance here is to understand that your emotional brain has developed very little in comparison to other parts of your brain, and will react to much less significant situations in the same primitive way. An example could be, filling out a job application form. One of the questions isn't clear so you're not sure what answer they want. Even though you are aware that you can complete the form and you are not in any danger no matter what answer you give, you are likely to feel frustration, apprehension and even anger. Your perception of the situation has been distorted and magnified. To be more specific, the emotional brain will shine a spotlight on this inconvenience, so you place all your energy there and disregard everything else in the hope that you take whatever action is required so you have the answer they want. The significant motive behind this is the second prime directive which is to **avoid failure**. Once again in a primitive world we were hunters. We had to become successful hunters in order to survive. If we continually failed, we would starve. This of course isn't the way we live today, but to the primitive emotional brain failure is potentially life threatening. What creates even greater quantities of anxiety is when others are aware of your failure. This explains the third prime directive which is the **need to be part of a group**, the emotional brain believes there is safety in numbers. If you are about to take your test have you told anyone? If you have, do you wish you could reverse that decision? If you could take your test as many times as you wished and no one would have any idea how many times you failed would that feel much easier? The strong possibility is that it would. The emotional brain feels that you need to be a part of a group or more specifically a successful or important member of a group. This greatly increases your chances of remaining there, where you are protected with a much better chance of survival. At this moment you may be asking, "wouldn't life be easier without the emotional brain?" The initial response may be yes, however it's worth remembering that your emotions are not all challenging ones. When you pass your test imagine the feelings of excitement, pride and overwhelming happiness. Any mission worth having will come with obstacles and challenges. It's the challenges that make the mission worth having, so don't wish they weren't there. Instead learn how to work with your emotional brain and use its huge energy to propel you forward so you can achieve life's biggest missions, enjoy this moment and it starts with passing your test.

- **The primitive emotional brain is designed primarily to keep you safe and alive.**
- **Its prime directives are, fight or flight response. To avoid failure and to be a valued member of a group.**

A New Way of Thinking

The majority of people believe their emotions are a direct response to their senses. In other words, they see, hear, touch, smell or taste something, and an emotion is generated that's in line with the information they have received. We have already touched on this so let's delve a little deeper and explain further why this is incorrect. Let's assume there are three people who are taken to a theme park. They arrive at the fastest, highest roller coaster in the park. As they step back and look at the ride, all three see the same ride however they all have very different perceptions. The first person looks with excitement and says, "Wow, this is incredible." The second person holds their breath, steps back and says, "Oh no, this is my worst nightmare!" The third person tilts their head up, places their hands in their pockets and with a tone of disinterest says, "Is that it, just a silly park ride?" This demonstrates that there's a missing component in most people's model that creates their perceptions and ignites their emotions. The missing component is what I call *programs*. Our programs are what makes us individuals. They include our beliefs, decisions, attitudes, experiences and most importantly our language. Although we all have the same programs, the data loaded in them is vastly different for all of us. The data is collected over our lifetime and up until now I'm sure for most people it has gone undetected. The revised model now looks like this: We accept raw information from our five senses, and this is processed in our programs. The programs compare this information from our past experiences and present perceptions before the filtered information is then fed to the emotional brain. The emotional brain produces an emotion that's in line with the information it received from the programs, not our senses. Once we have an emotion it's likely we will perform a behaviour which will generate a result. We can't change our emotional brain but we can reload the data that's stored in the programs. By doing this we can change the emotional brain's responses that drive our behaviours. This places us at a new level of responsibility and of course in much more control of our results. Let's look at a scenario that explains how programs work.

Katy's lessons are progressing well so her instructor decides to take a different route where she will drive through a heavily populated area. She begins the lesson well and feels relaxed, when without any warning a pedestrian walks out in front of her. She panics, freezes and the instructor takes control of the car by slamming on the brakes. There is a moment of silence before the pedestrian carries on walking as nothing had happened. The instructor smiles and says, "not your fault, just take it as an experience." Although his words were intended to regain a calm atmosphere, she is clearly shocked. Katy's next lesson begins well, and she is good spirits. Once again, she is instructed to take a different route where she approaches a junction which is positioned at the top of a steep hill. She applies the hand brake and waits patiently for the passing traffic to clear; she notices in her rear-view mirror a car pulling up very close behind her. The driver looks uncomfortable as he taps his steering wheel and seems to mouth some words directed at her. She turns her attention to the situation she faces and has a clear path to move forward, however this is a hill start and she is aware of the car that's just inches from her back bumper. With this in mind, coupled with the look of impatience on the drivers face she loses her focus and stalls the engine. Her instructor calmly says, "no problem, all in your own time." She makes a second attempt and once again misjudges her clutch control and stalls. The driver behind beeps his horn and she can hear his calls for her to "get moving!" At this point she would do anything to avoid this intensely uncomfortable situation and begins to feel extremely distressed. Although this situation is clearly upsetting, it's what's happening at an unconscious level that is more important. Her programs are collecting and storing information based on her perceptions of the past events. These suggest that driving is stressful with hidden hazards and offensive people everywhere. The real danger is that when she prepares for further lessons or sits in the driver's seat, her emotional brain receives information from her programs that provide guidance with regard to the event. The programs' data suggests a strong possibility of an experience filled with fear and distress. Remember her emotional brain's number one priority is to keep her safe, and will respond by filling her mind with anxiety, nerves and even physical sickness if necessary. In fact, it will do whatever it needs to prevent her from taking any further lessons. This way she avoids any risk and remains safe.

These unwanted emotions are completely natural; the good news is that she can reload the programs and experience a vastly different response from the emotional brain, and it's much easier than you may think. Let the changes begin.

- **Programs receive information from our senses.**
- **The emotional brain is fed the processed information from the programs.**
- **We can re-load the programs and change the reactions of the emotional brain.**

Words Are Powerful

The importance of our words is far greater than you may think. When you hear the words: social media, education, friends, or bar, you have to create pictures and movies in your mind to make sense of what's being said. You won't always be consciously aware of it, however this is key. Words don't necessarily describe your reality but they do create it. As we have already discovered three people can experience the same event yet have completely different emotions. The way you describe a situation not only has an effect on that moment in time, it loads information into your programs that will have a long-term effect. Becoming conscious of the way you describe situations alone will have a positive impact. Imagine you have a driving instructor who makes little eye contact. He rarely smiles and as soon as you step into the car, he instantly explains what the lesson will focus on. No small talk, little eye contact, no pleasantries, just straight onto the job in hand. You may describe him as unfriendly with little or no people skills. These comments can only produce a movie in your mind of someone you would rather not spend time with. Someone with no personality and one who perhaps doesn't want to spend time making you feel relaxed. You may conclude he is unhappy in his job. You could however describe the situation very differently. He may be so focused on his task of teaching he doesn't want to waste time talking. He wants to invest every minute on the most important person in the car which of course is you. He may be shy and finds that putting all his attention on his work helps him place all the focus on the lesson rather than him. So, you actually have an instructor who has one purpose which is to put his heart and soul into his mission, which is for you to pass your test as quickly as possible saving you time and money. This revised version will load the information relating to the instructor into the programs, this is fed to the emotional brain which produces a more supportive response whenever you have a lesson.

A friend who has developed a very successful building company is well known for his upbeat state and incredible sense of humour. I asked him how he remains in this state during difficult economic times. He smiled and, in his words, "It's all a game." He explained that he always refers to the building industry in this way. His responsibility is to make bids for contracts, and must ensure that he includes costs of labour, materials and profit. He had suffered severe anxiety when he was younger and had also experienced a failed business venture where he lost a considerable amount of money and more importantly his mental stability. He told me that he is now a player/manager. His role is to play each game to the best of his ability. If it all goes wrong all his employees (Players in his words) understand that he pours all of his experience and energy into every game, and he will do everything possible for his team to triumph. I believe this is an important lesson for us all.

Changing the words we use to describe a situation or experience that would normally create anxiety is easy, and can be personalised. Do you find that the word *test* sends an uneasy feeling through your body? The word test for many is a reminder of school exams where expectation and nerves are felt at high levels. Although there is some help available in school to remain calm, it's rarely enough and the air of importance outweighs it many times over. When the word changes, so do the internal pictures. Instead of using the words *driving test* you could call it a *driving meeting*. Notice how different it feels when you think of a meeting rather than a test. Any name that works for you is fine, but I will continue for the remainder of the book using the term *driving meeting*. Another term that may need to be altered is the name we give the examiner. The word 'examiner' may conjure up negative connotations of cliché and passed on experiences. You could use any term you wish but for the purpose of the book I will rename the examiner the *scorer*. The job of the scorer is to sit beside you, give you a few instructions and keep score. Of course, others that speak to you won't change these words, so reframe them for yourself when they use them or ask them to follow you with your choice of names.

By making these small changes you are perceiving and reloading important data in the programs. Take some time to think how this could affect other situations in your life? How often do you speak to people without any thought of how powerful your words are? Understanding the words you use has a profound effect on the emotional brain. It makes sense that you could not only use different words to describe a person or situation, you could also exclude words and notice a vastly different reaction emotionally. Going back to the way you describe your driving lessons, what words or phrases do you currently use when you feel nervous? You perhaps see the instructor pull up outside and automatically say, "oh god here we go, please don't mess up!" Already you will now know what the pictures in your mind are going to look like. Saying the words "mess up" can only produce an internal image of a lesson going wrong. This is likely to generate feelings in your body that we all identify as nerves, anxiety or apprehension.

I was working with a group of athletes and asked them to create a situation, event or scenario in their mind which would produce negative emotions. I then asked them to do something very different. As soon as the feelings were evident, I wanted them to avoid labelling these unwanted feelings, essentially, they would mute their internal voice. This prevented any further pictures or movie developing in their mind. They would simply notice the feelings without words or judgement. These sensations were then only chemical feelings in their body. Most explained that they would normally feel a heavy uneasy feeling in their stomach which without thought would be labelled as an anxious or nervous feeling. By excluding any words, the feeling diminished and drifted away in seconds. When we label a physical feeling, we give it oxygen and life. When we remove the label, it becomes nothing more than a chemical feeling in the body. After the feeling had disappeared, we could look at the situation or event that had produced those unwanted feelings and describe it with words and phrases that promoted excitement, confidence and assurance. It took the athletes some conscious effort to master this; ultimately, they were changing a strategy that had become habitual, so it was going to take some time and effort to rectify. A number of them expressed a difficulty in muting their internal voice. I suggested they pressed their tongue into the roof of their mouth. When we self-talk we usually move our tongue as we would if we were talking out loud. Pressing your tongue into the roof of the mouth prevents this from happening. Those who were serious about taking control of their state stayed on track and described the changes that occurred over time as astonishing. All these skills are easy and in many cases common sense. The thought of becoming a different person (emotionally) may for some sound overwhelming, but essentially you are just making a few decisions on a consistent basis.

As you know your emotional brain is designed to keep you safe and alive. It's constantly on the lookout for potential problems. It can steal your focus in a heartbeat. Fear is the number one attention grabber. You will instinctively focus on fear, to ensure you are constantly aware of it. When faced with a challenging situation it's likely you at least contemplate the difficulty or the possibility of failure and for some even focus on it completely. One of the ways this is accomplished will be the questions you contemplate after a poor driving lesson; you may ask yourself, "why am I such a poor driver?" This is one we have all asked and the answers can only create a miserable picture that lowers your self-belief. Asking better questions is vital. An example could be, "how can I become an outstanding driver?" Or an even better question could be, "how can I become an outstanding driver and relish the process?" In order to answer this, you must search for ways you can accomplish both parts of the question. Practising the ideas and reloading your programs will enable you to enjoy stepping out of your comfort zone during situations that once felt uncomfortable. Remember everything you experience is a perception that you have control over. Whenever you catch yourself asking poor questions where the answer can only take you to a negative outcome, stop immediately and reframe it so the answers produce intrigue and possibility. One more point regarding questions, make sure you always ask yourself what you want and never what you don't want. Have you ever felt overwhelmed and told yourself or someone "I don't care about the details I just don't want to fail"? That may sound like an obvious thing to say, after all you certainly don't want to fail. The problem with this sentence is that your mind cannot process negatives, so you must run the scenario of failing to then know that's not what you want. If I said, "whatever you do don't think of a big pink elephant with huge pink ears and a trunk", you have to visualise it first to then carry out the request to not think of it. Always request what you do want and never what you don't want. Remember your mind cannot process negatives, so make it easy. The revised comment to yourself or the person in the conversation could be, "I'm putting all my focus on everything I need to pass, and I'm really looking forward to it," making sure you adopt the physiology of certainty with a smile.

Practising is essential, after all you are changing the habits of a lifetime. Another component regarding your language which is equally important is the *tone* you use when you are talking to yourself. When anxiety strikes it's probable that the tone of voice changes to one of hesitation and retreat. When did you last successfully confront a demanding task with hesitation and doubt? Our choice of words is critical but also the tone of our internal voice will generate certainty. Let me introduce to you a new friend. It's your new inner voice which will become your coach and new best friend. Your inner coach will only use words of necessity with a tone of complete certainty. Imagine the characteristics of your coach. When I work with sports individuals and teams, we call the inner coach the Sgt Major. They will create a vision of their Sgt Major. Most will imagine a figure of intensity and focus. Someone who picks you up when you are exhausted and guides you to the outcome you desire. Produce an image of power, force and energy. Your Sgt Major accepts total responsibility without excuses. He attacks any fear with an inner strength that we all have, although few ever access. Take your time designing the ultimate Sgt Major. Helping a runner in the production of her Sgt Major inner voice, we discussed a reoccurring situation she faced during competition. Her target was to run the marathon for her country. Unfortunately, when her main rival was close to her during the latter stages of a race, she would feel her energy draining and a sense of uncertainty develop. I expressed the importance of her inner voice and the advantages the Sgt Major would bring. She was very enthusiastic but found it difficult to replicate it, so I adopted a different approach. I knew she was a mother to a seven-year-old daughter to whom she was completely devoted. I gave her a scenario to contemplate. If her daughter was in immediate danger and she had to run a mile to save her what would her inner voice say? Her physiology changed immediately as she said, "I'm coming and nothing on this planet will stop me!" I asked her to remember the tone of her internal voice along with the sense of authority, this was *her* Sgt Major inner voice. Since our discussion she has run for England on several occasions and describes her Sgt Major as the definitive inner coach.

Another athlete who was an outstanding talent placed every ounce of effort into our sessions. After a disappointing event he revealed that he feared certain athletes. He explained that whenever he was competing against American or Jamaican athletes, he felt inferior. When I asked where this came from, he said "they are huge, very muscular and dominating." He went on to tell me that he looks at them, then back to himself and internally voices, "I'm tiny, weak and nothing compared to them!" As he explained this to me his physiology was shrinking by the second and his voice was becoming very weak. I stood up and invited him to do the same. We then created his inner coach which adopted a very different internal voice. When he next competed, he arrived on the track and this time his inner coach was fully present. He looked at the other competitors which triggered his inner coach to say to them (only within himself), "You are here to push me to my limits, I don't care who you are, what you have won and how many medals you have, I will produce a performance that's going to destroy you all." If at any time he felt any evidence of anxiety his inner voice would say, "I don't have time for this, get out of my face. I have a job to do and that's to produce a performance that will destroy the field, humiliate all competitors if I have to!"

You may be thinking this all sounds a bit over the top, but the reality is, when you place all your attention on an all-out attack on the fear and drive towards your desired performance you become the non-negotiable assassin. The probability of you succeeding increases dramatically. Although the athlete made incredible progress by completely changing the data in the programs it was vital that he spoke to me (or someone else) about his anxieties. It's often perceived that we shouldn't talk about our feelings, and this is most common in young men. When you verbally 'let it all out' you will feel a huge sense of relief. When anxiety builds, we must have a way of releasing it. Find someone who will listen to you. Unfortunately, most people listen for a short time with the sole purpose to reply and express their own problems. Find a close friend, relative or someone you trust and make an agreement that when either of you need to talk the other person will simply listen. This increases trust and helps build a solid friendship. A good friend of mine was in most people's eyes a workaholic. His ambition and drive to succeed was ferocious, he was well known as the guy who would take on huge tasks and responsibilities. After a short period of time his mental health began to suffer and it was evident that something had to change. The first step was to speak to someone whenever he felt tension building. He explained that this simply wasn't feasible, others in his office were too busy with their own pressures to listen to him. I suggested that during his lunch break he should turn his phone off (to avoid any embarrassment of it ringing), place the phone to his ear and pretend he was having a conversation as he went for a walk. The one-way conversation would allow him to let it all out and voice his concerns, frustrations and anger. During this period, he was releasing the tension he had built up allowing him to use better language patterns to reload the data in his programs. As a result, his frustration and anger are far less frequent, and he now has a plan in place when they occur. Another commonly used method is to write down your feelings and worries. I urge you to take this advice, this is your health and wellbeing. Life is precious so look after yourself and live every minute.

- **Words create our reality.**
- **'Driving test' becomes 'driving meeting'.**
- **'Instructor' becomes the 'scorer'.**
- **Avoid negative labels.**
- **Ask better questions.**
- **Sgt Major inner voice.**
- **Release anxiety by talking.**

The World of Visualisation

From this point you will need to become familiar with a technique that I'm sure you have heard of but never fully understood its incredible benefits. The technique is visualisation, and whilst for some it will feel very natural, many will find it more challenging and often the frustration becomes too much and they quit, denying themselves an incredible psychological skill. If you are proficient with visualisation you can skip this short chapter and dive straight into the next one. For everyone else, this will be a very helpful exercise to assist in mastering this essential skill. You simply need somewhere quiet to practise for as little as ten minutes a day. If you have ever attempted visualisation and found it difficult, then I'm sure you will agree ten minutes a day will be time well spent.

Find an everyday object, an example could be a coffee mug. Look at it closely for around ten seconds then close your eyes and bring the image into your mind for a further ten seconds. Now open your eyes and repeat until you can recall the image without any difficulty. Once you feel comfortable continue the process but this time notice more detail with your eyes open. It could be the detailed pattern on the mug or perhaps any imperfections on the handle. Once you have gathered further details repeat the previous steps. Practise this daily for as little as ten minutes until you can comfortably recall the image in detail at will. Once this is accomplished you will be ready to experience one of the most underrated psychological skills.

- **Focus on a single object, close your eyes and bring back the image in your mind.**
- **Repeat the process.**

A Virtual Experience

We have already highlighted the importance of changing the story we produce in our minds. Although everyone will have different degrees of success to begin with, when mastered you will have a superpower. It may be tempting to underestimate its importance, but for those who decide to follow all the ideas, they will drastically reduce self-doubt and the restrictions that most people are bombarded with from every angle of their lives. Your brain is undeniably the most incredible creation imaginable, however a remarkable fact is, that it cannot differentiate between an event that actually happens and one that is vividly imagined. This is significant and we will use this imperfection to our advantage. You may have heard people say that they have problems imagining a successful completion to a future event because in their words "they cannot see it." Although this is a metaphor, it's true. Sports competitors often report an inner vision where they see the successful completion of a shot, throw or pass in their minds a second or two before they actually execute it. This translates into a feeling, which we call confidence. This is key as it demonstrates how an image or movie in your mind influences the desired result.

For those who are sceptical, let's put an exercise in place. Stand up straight and raise an arm and point your finger straight out in front of you. If it's safe to do so with your feet planted on the spot twist your body from your waist up as far as you can comfortably go. Make a note of how far you went before returning to the original position, now lower your arm and close your eyes. Next visualise raising the same arm whilst pointing your finger straight ahead. Keep this focus and imagine turning your body the same way but this time you can turn much further. On this occasion you are turning an additional 25% before returning to the starting position. Repeat this imagined experience again but this time your body turns 50% further, before returning to the original starting position. Finally repeat the process one more time whilst imagining your body turning with ease a complete 360 degrees. Allow yourself a few seconds to recover and open your eyes. Now physically raise your arm and point your finger straight ahead. Turn your body from the waist up as far as you can without any discomfort. The vast majority will notice this time they can physically turn much further. Why is this? In simple terms you have now seen what's possible. You have fast tracked a new belief; you have seen it so you can believe it.

You may be aware that sports competitors often use visualisation. You now have a guide to visualisation, but we live in a world where we experience events with more than a visual representation, so it's vital to include sounds and feelings. This is called mental rehearsal. By experiencing an event consistently in your mind, you will accept the experience in the same way as if it occurred in the material world. This loads new data into the belief program extremely efficiently. It's time to become the producer and director of your internal movie. This movie is how you want the experience to unfold. This will load data into the programs that promote enthusiasm, confidence and self-belief. A suggested movie could be observing the 'scorer' approach you. Instinctively you become aware of your strong confident posture. Your breathing is deep and comfortable as you smile. As you step into the car your attention is on the job in hand. You place your focus on every word the scorer says whilst making sure you are sat comfortably. Your internal coach (Sgt Major) is ready to abolish any negative dialogue or feelings, ensuring your state is one of extreme focus and self-belief. You feel so alive and assertive as you demonstrate the ultimate driving performance and enjoy every moment.

Brainwaves in adults alter during the day so practising early morning or late evening will result in less resistance from your critical thinking brain. To rehearse the new movie and begin the process you will need to drift into a relaxed state. For obvious reasons you should only attempt this exercise when you can fully relax and ignore everything that is happening around you. Never perform this exercise when driving, operating any machinery or carrying out any task that requires your focus and concentration. Find a space where you can ignore the outside world. Turn off your phone and any other distractions. Sit on a high-backed chair so you are sat upright with your back straight. You may find wearing a pair of headphones without any music helps block out any external noise. Initially take in some deep breaths. Breath in slowly through your nose and exhale through your mouth, continue this for around a minute. Now place your attention to the top of your head and imagine just above you is a bright white light. This light is the light of relaxation. In just a moment it will slowly move from the top of your head to the tips of your toes, instantly relaxing each part it comes in contact with. This requires some imagination but it's something we can all do with practise. Simply become conscious of this imaginary light moving slowly and gently through your body, noticing each group of muscles relaxing with ease. You may find you fall asleep to begin with but with practise you will be able to reach a relaxed state between being awake and being asleep. Once you have reached this state simply replay the movie you created and relive it. See the event through your own eyes and make sure the movie is big, bright and colourful. Include any important sounds and turn up all the positive emotions. Mental rehearsal may to some seem a little over the top to pass your driving test but as you are about to learn, the belief program will require a new exciting movie. Practising mental rehearsal three to four times a week will provide those who embrace it with life changing results. When all of these skills and techniques are combined it's astonishing how your state changes when you need it the most. I'm sure you have heard the saying, "I'll believe it when I see it." However, when you believe it you will have a much greater chance of seeing it.

- **Enter a relaxed state.**
- **Design a mind movie.**
- **Movie of you driving with authority, confidence and enjoyment.**
- **Movie is big, bright and colourful.**

You Can Do Anything (Beliefs)

If you believe you can, or you believe you can't, you are absolutely right. Beliefs have a huge bearing on outcomes and achievements. What you believe to be possible will decide if or how you take on any task and what level of enthusiasm you apply. Every day you complete some extremely complex activities without any hesitation or second thoughts. Walking is something most take for granted; we rarely if ever stop to think of how we do this without falling over. There are countless calculations that have to be made with each step. Essentially, we have a cast iron belief that we can execute this task and it's become an unconscious habit. The question is, how are beliefs created? Many of your beliefs are generated when you are very young. You receive the information from parents, carers and teachers. You listen, gather and accept it to be true. The big questions are, how do you change your beliefs?

Fortunately, there are techniques we can use that collectively will change your beliefs regarding what you are capable of. Most people never understand this, and go through life with very limiting beliefs. As a result, they never achieve anything near to their full potential. This is nothing short of a tragedy, and I urge you to read this book at least three times and practise the ideas consistently so you do something extraordinary, which is to pass with confidence, to develop true self-belief and then use these skills in every area of your life to achieve what you are really capable of. The first lesson in the production of a new set of beliefs is to become selective about whom you listen to. You will hear other people's beliefs every minute of the day. Some will say your driving test will be extremely scary no matter what you do. They have experienced this and believe that to be true for everyone. They may say it to help you prepare or in the hope that you don't get your hopes up. After all, how will you feel if you fail? By making you aware of the difficulty now you won't be so disappointed if it happens.

Make a decision that you will listen to conversations differently from now. Your friends and family will give you their advice, however their advice is their beliefs not yours. This isn't about being disrespectful but rather laying a pathway for your future without limitations. As we have already mentioned, the biggest stealer of your attention is fear. When you are faced with fear, you will instinctively pay careful attention to anything that could physically or emotionally harm you, so it's important to focus on what you want and not on what you don't want. After a conversation where you have been told the countless number of ways you will be terrified leading up to and during the event, you may find that you do something that is incredibly damaging, and you must avoid it at all cost. After the conversation you may rehearse what was said and it's probable you will focus on the fear by going into the detail of all the distressing parts in your mind multiple times. When this occurs, you are loading the belief program with data that suggests the whole experience will be intensely stressful. So how can this be dealt with?

After any conversation where you feel apprehension, it's important to take time and contemplate if the information is a fact or a belief (most of the time it will be a belief). For the apprehension to be present you will have a story, or to be specific, a movie in your mind. The first point that must be dealt with is to change the movie. If it has been present for a while, we will need to erase it or at least tone it down. This is a simple step by step process:

- Step one - if you see the events through your own eyes (first position) imagine floating out of your body so you are now watching it as a spectator.

- Step two - you must drain the energy by muting any sounds and freeze frame the movie, so it becomes a still picture.

- Step three – drain any colour from the picture so its black and white, then shrink the picture down so it's a fraction of its original size and finally imagine the picture exploding.

You may need to practise this several times until you find the old emotions have diminished. You already have a new movie (created during the mental rehearsal chapter) which highlights your high energy, focused state. This movie includes what you see (through your own eyes), hear and feel. The movie is bright, colourful and the instructions are clear, with the feelings of assurance fully present. This movie when repeated consistently over days will begin to load new data into the belief program. Over time you will enjoy a very different belief. The most important point to remember is our acceptance of the story (our movie) regarding who we are and what we can achieve. In time we act out this behaviour, so the story becomes true, we become the person in the movie. We generally accomplish what the movies suggests, so I invite you to stop and contemplate how powerful this is as you become the author, director and producer of the upgraded version. This is time well spent so place your efforts into producing your very best work. As you analyse the movie you will notice that it's based purely on your performance, as you know this will provide you with the best possible outcome.

I was asked to assist a man in his late twenties who had failed his driving test five times. His instructor expressed his disbelief that this had happened on so many occasions. When I met the student, he spoke openly about his anguish and his desperation to finally pass. What I told him certainly wasn't what he was expecting to hear. I explained that his job was NOT to pass. He frowned, stared at me and said, "Can you repeat that please?" Again, I explain that his job was NOT to pass his test. He leaned forward and said abruptly, "What are you talking about! Why are you even here?" I then continued, "Your job is to listen to each individual request and execute each one to the very best of your ability. If you are asked to take the next left turn you follow that request taking care to perform that instruction to the best of your ability. Once you have completed that task, you place all your attention on the next request. So, it's not about passing this huge obstacle that you call a driving test, that's the outcome. It's your job to listen to each individual command and execute each one to the best of your ability. If you have ambitions to win multiple Olympic titles, that's your outcome. Every day you go to work and focus on the training that will bring Olympic glory. The reality is that if you can be 100% confident that you can listen to an instruction and follow that instruction to the best of your ability, you will step into the car with 100% confidence. You accept that the result isn't completely within your control but your performance is. In a nutshell, control what you can instead of becoming stressed trying to control what you can't. This new thought process had a dramatic effect on the student: he passed at his next attempt. The way we process information is key to the way it's loaded in the programs and the way that information is then fed to the emotional brain.

I now urge you to expect to drive well no matter what. I understand that this can be challenging, we all have pessimists amongst our family and friends who may say, "If I expect it to go wrong, I can only be pleasantly surprised." This is common but completely the wrong way of tackling any task that's worthwhile. Firstly, people who are pessimistic are fearful. Their focus is directed on their fear, and they are constantly aware of it whilst hoping that they may avoid it. Another saying is, "What you seek you shall find." In other words what you look for, you will discover. If your focus is on an experience going badly wrong, you increase the chances of it becoming reality. When you make an attempt to do something it's almost inevitable you will look out for problems. When you focus on what you want and go for it with conviction, any potential barriers are far less likely to appear. From this point forward expect to drive to your full potential; this alone will boost your chances of success.

Changing a belief can of course take time and practise. During this change you will face situations where you automatically respond in the old way because the new data hasn't yet taken over. To help you during this period I have a hack that will help change your state rapidly. When you find yourself doubting your ability, perhaps you are minutes from a driving lesson, follow this plan to redirect the poor state to a desirable one in seconds. Firstly, close your eyes and imagine a set of traffic lights. Initially look at the red light and say to yourself, "Stop." This gives an order to your mind to stop the current thinking process. Then notice the amber light and voice internally, "Get ready." Finally pay attention to the green light and shout to yourself, "GO!" Now make the alterations to your physiology, bring in your Sgt Major and give yourself direct orders to attack the fear, check your physiology is strong so you feel a positive assertive state.

Let me explain how I used this when I was asked to attend a networking party. A friend sent me a picture of a man who was also attending and suggested that I made a connection with him. In my friends' words, "If you only talk to one person make sure it's this guy. He has all the contacts you need." I was extremely grateful and then asked, "What's he like?" My friend paused and said with a less than enthusiastic tone that he wasn't a particularly nice person, in fact he can be quite aggressive, but not to worry about all that, just have a chat.

Anyone who knows me will tell you that I will avoid aggression at all costs, but this was important, so I attended the meeting. When I arrived there were only a few people there, so I made my way to the bar. As I looked around the room, I instantly noticed my contact. He was alone and was paying all his attention to his phone. There was once a time when I would automatically have made a hundred excuses not to walk over to him, such as, it's a bit early, I'll do it later, or he's on his phone and the last thing he wants is me pouncing on him within the first few minutes. But I have a very different mindset now, and I expect to do all things that are within my control to make my mission a reality, so I followed the traffic light system. I closed my eyes and imagined the traffic lights. I looked at the red and said to myself with my Sgt Major tone, "Stop!" Then noticing the amber, I internally voiced "Get ready." Then looking at the green light I shouted to myself "GO!" I checked my physiology making sure I stood tall, shoulders back with my head held high. Every step was one of conviction and my Sgt Major voice said with a commanding tone, "Get over to him, shake his hand and make sure he knows who you are and exactly how you can help each other." I repeated this as I marched across the room. I caught his eye, put out my hand and introduced myself. We had a fifteen-minute chat and we exchanged contact details. I walked away and congratulated myself. This is extremely important to do, although you may find it difficult at first. When you give yourself praise you will find that you naturally feel happier and increase your self-belief. Any time you step out of your comfort zone is an act of courage. Greater courage will result in more confidence.

Make sure you acknowledge this to yourself and remember to smile. After the party I found that he wasn't the contact my friend had portrayed, but I did what I needed to do and that was by far the most important part of the exercise.

Working with sports individuals and teams, it became clear to me that some have such high levels of anxiety leading up to competitions that they could be compared to having a phobia. Often their breathing would become fast and shallow, their heart rate would increase, and their minds seemed to hit the panic button. Often this happened without any warning and was described by some as a full-on panic attack. This is a terrifying experience and I'm sure this has happened to some of you. This can occur any time and for those it affects this is immensely important, so please read carefully. During my work I have adopted a skill which takes you from high levels of anxiety to excitement in seconds. The technique is called the rapid change technique. We have already highlighted that your brain is ingenious beyond imagination. As you know it cannot differentiate between an event that actually happens and an event that is vividly imagined. It's also equally important to understand that anxiety generates a faster heart rate, creates a sensation of butterflies in the stomach and builds tension in the body. Similarly, when you encounter high levels of excitement, it's usual to experience a faster heart rate, butterflies in the stomach and tension in the body. The feelings of anxiety are the same as the feelings of excitement. This is vital to comprehend and allows you to make incredible modifications to your emotions. The first step is recognising the trigger.

Let's make an assumption that you are sitting at home waiting for the instructor to take you to the test centre, this is the trigger. The second step is to become imaginative and design and produce a movie in your mind. This movie is the successful completion of the task. The movie must include what you see, hear and feel and must generate excitement. The movie could be that you are looking at the scorer with the feeling of shaking her hand as she smiles and says, "Congratulations, you have passed!" It doesn't matter what the movie is, as long as it shows a successful completion of the task that was creating anxiety but now produces excitement. We also need what we call a state break. This seamlessly takes the rise of the negative feelings and switches it so it becomes excitement. To achieve this, we will once again use the set of traffic lights. Let's put it all together so you can see it in action:

You are sat at home waiting for the instructor to arrive when the anxiety rises quickly. Firstly, close your eyes and imagine the traffic lights. Notice the red light and with a tone of authority say to yourself "STOP!" Pay attention to the amber light and voice to yourself, "Get ready." Finally focus on the green light and say loudly to yourself, "GO!" Bring in the new movie and notice the smile on the scorers face as she says, "Congratulations! You have passed!" Imagine the feeling of shaking her hand. Now the important part, say to yourself with your Sgt Major commanding tone, "I feel amazing, I'm so excited!" Your emotional brain will link the exciting movie to the physical feelings, accept they match and allow the excitement to continue. The first time you do this the effect may last only for a few minutes so you will need to repeat the process. In time you will find that the positive emotions take over. This skill is one of the most valuable to have in your locker. Here is the summary of the rapid change technique.

1. Become aware of the situations where you are likely to feel extremely anxious.

2. Remember that the physical feelings of anxiety are a faster heart rate, butterflies in the stomach and tension in the body. The physical feelings of excitement are the same.

3. Create a movie in your mind that portrays a successful completion to the driving lesson or test.

4. The new movie must include exciting pictures, feelings and sounds.

5. The moment the anxiety rises, close your eyes and imagine the traffic lights. Observe the red light and say to yourself "STOP!" Look at the amber light and internally voice "Get ready." Finally notice the green light and shout to yourself "GO!"

6. Run the new movie in your mind. Make sure it's big, bright and loud. See the event through your own eyes.

7. Using the Sgt Major commanding tone, voice loudly to yourself, "I feel amazing, I'm so excited!"

8. The emotional brain links the exciting movie to the

physical feelings, accepts they match, and allows it to continue.

9. Check your physiology and ensure that it's one of complete certainty.

10. It's highly likely you will have to repeat this a few times, however the more you do the faster it initiates and the longer the effect lasts. Practise this for any situations in your life where you may feel high levels of anxiety, so there will be a faster response when you need it.

As you can see, it's not the event that creates the anxiety, it's the meaning attached to it. I'm sure you are now beginning to understand you cannot always change the situation but you can always alter your beliefs. When you put all this together with a physiology of confidence you are making huge strides towards becoming the master of your emotions, behaviours and results. The future is very exciting.

- **Peoples negative beliefs are theirs, not yours.**
- **Unwanted beliefs: eradicate the old mind movie first.**
- **New belief, rehearse new mind movie.**
- **It's not your job to pass, it's your job to execute each instruction to the best of your ability.**
- **Expect to drive well.**
- **Quick response hack, use traffic light system.**
- **Rapid change technique.**

The Hidden Gems

You may have experienced an unsuccessful conclusion to previous "driving meetings", and no matter what occurred it's probable that you now have some level of apprehension regarding the next attempt. As you now know your emotional brain will avoid failure. The possibility of failing in front of a familiar group multiple times will really fire it up, so it's vital to learn what failure really is. Firstly, success is a wonderful feeling, but a very poor teacher. We often watch the world's most successful people with huge admiration and assume they are natural born winners. They seem immune to the anxieties that mere mortals suffer. Of course, the reality is that we rarely get to witness the blood, sweat and tears they had to endure in order to enjoy their success. Your experience program has a huge influence over your emotions. When the data is loaded with heart-breaking moments where your perception of events is embarrassing and often humiliating, the emotional brain will accept the information and produce an emotion that's designed to stop you in your tracks, thus avoiding a recurrence of the same situation. When this happens, you miss out on life's most exciting and worthwhile experiences. A past experience is merely a movie in your mind that can be altered to create a different understanding. A new movie can fuel the emotional brain to produce considerable excitement when taking on a challenge with greater knowledge and skills.

The problem with a negative view of a past experience is that you will focus on a failure with intent and great awareness. Where you place your focus is where you direct your thoughts. Failure is of course something we all want to avoid however all experiences are packed with valuable ways we can learn. A golden rule to remember is, 'There is no failure, only feedback.' It's natural to think that success is what creates happiness and although this is true, consistent growth creates true fulfilment and long-term happiness. If you have failed once, twice or multiple times, what was the first thing you did when you were told that you had failed? It's likely that you went over the event in your mind. Maybe you were asked what went wrong? You contemplate the question and in order to answer it you must go over all the details that are now upsetting and which fills the programs with unhelpful data. Instead you need to ask yourself a very different question. The question is, "How many ways can I improve my performance?" This pre-supposes that there are many ways you can implement changes that significantly increase the chances of success next time. I suggest you write them down, never use your mind as a filling cabinet. Share your ideas with your instructor so you can add to them over time. It's vital to internalise the fact that you are learning, growing and becoming an accomplished driver. Never see a second, third or fourth attempt as an accumulation but simply apply all your attention to the one you are taking. Gather all the learning from past experiences and move forward. Use the mental rehearsal technique and produce a movie where you have included all the improvements you have identified and run this movie through your mind regularly. It's easy and natural to recall past events for reasons we have already covered, but as you will discover in the following chapter, living in the moment will help produce a laser focus. Remember it's important to know the desired outcome, but you must place your attention on the performance. Sometimes situations occur that you have little or no control over. Although these circumstances are certainly challenging and difficult, you must accept it's not always your fault that failure occurs, but it's always your responsibility how you react to it. When you take control over your thoughts you become the master of your mind. This is a very powerful place to be and one few people ever experience.

- **We learn from failure.**

Attitude and Focus

From an early age people measure our chances for success by our attitude. Attitude can mean something different to us all. How much more do you achieve when in your eyes you have a great attitude towards it? Do you spot a positive attitude in others? We can list some ingredients of a great attitude with a strong physiology, an eagerness to achieve success, a strong internal voice and a controlled focus. In NLP there is a saying, 'Energy flows where focus goes.' One important aspect for a great attitude is how effective we are at blocking outside interference. The capacity to produce focus with intent is a valuable skill for anyone. During my years in sport I've often heard coaches tell their students to focus on an area, golfers to place the ball or footballers to pass the ball in a certain area. Often this area is of a considerable size. I prefer to be very specific. I ask tennis players to imagine they will serve the ball on a specific spot, or snooker and pool players to position the white ball on a chalk mark. A rugby player once told me when he kicks the ball between the posts, he imagines a spectator in the crowd who is sat exactly between the two posts. The spectator is holding a bottle of water. His task is to kick the ball so it knocks the water bottle out of the spectator's hand. The chances of him missing the conversion and kicking the ball outside the posts has been significantly reduced. So, what's this got to do with passing your driving meeting? When you place your focus on a specific spot you reduce the possibility of focusing on anything else. I'm sure your instructor has said to you, "where you aim is where you will steer." When you look at a pedestrian or something that catches your eye, you instinctively steer towards it. From this moment, every task you execute must be methodical, measured and precise. When you sit in the car, stretch the seat belt slowly, ensuring you click it into the socket with accuracy. When you change gear make it as smooth as you can. When you steer around a corner take care to make your road positioning as precise as possible. I have a rule that all sports students must abide by. Pay attention to the details by ensuring everything is done to the very best of your ability.

When you place all your energy into the performance it's much easier to remain calm. It's very easy to do but easier not to do, so remain conscious of this. Focus is a psychological muscle and can be strengthened in the same way as a physical muscle in the form of exercise. A great exercise for increasing focus will require a quiet space, a book, headphones and some upbeat music. Place the headphones on and play some catchy music at low volume. Whilst it plays read a paragraph of the book. The aim is to read and comprehend what you have read whilst the music is playing. Once this feels comfortable gradually increase the volume. Continue this until the music is playing reasonably loudly and you are able to focus completely on the book and recall what you have read. This takes time and effort but generates an extremely strong focus muscle.

Anxiety is generally based on a past experience or a perceived future event that has or may go wrong. When you are in the moment it's more likely you will feel added control and positive energy. Being in the moment like all the other exercises requires practise and can be challenging to begin with. It doesn't need to be a set routine but rather a skill you rehearse whenever you have the opportunity, so try this additional exercise. This will complement the focus exercise and reinforce it. Initially place your focus on your breathing. Notice if you are breathing from the abdominal area or further upwards towards your chest. Is it shallow or deep? Remember deep abdominal breathing produces a calmer state. For one-minute pay attention to this pattern and nothing else. Although it's only a minute it can seem a lot longer and thoughts may enter your mind. The instinctive response will be to fight and attempt to get rid of them. This generally ends up with tension and frustration resulting in your enthusiasm deteriorating fast. Instead when any thoughts enter your mind accept them, then allow them to drift away as you refocus on your breathing. If you were talking to a friend in a busy coffee shop it's likely there will be many distractions. Other people talking, babies crying and the odd dispute amongst customers and staff. You could walk over to any one of these events and offer your assistance, however it's more likely that your attention is taken away for a short while and you then reconnect to the conversation with your friend. The exercise works in the same way; thoughts will make every attempt to take your focus, however the more you practise this the less thought distraction you will experience. After a time of exercising you will be able to extend the period of time focusing on your breathing. The desired outcome is to ground yourself and your thoughts at will. The focus exercise we looked at will greatly decrease the time to master this. When you are preparing to take a lesson, driving with your instructor or taking your driving meeting, the ability to remain in the present moment will be invaluable. Although you won't be focusing on your breathing, whilst driving you will of course be paying attention to each instruction you are given and executing that instruction to the very best of your ability, whilst blocking out all external interference. A phrase that has lived with me and one that I think will help you in this is, *wherever you are, be there.*

- **Energy flows where focus goes.**
- **Focus on your performance and be specific.**
- **Practise the focus exercise.**
- **Be in the moment.**

Summary

As you know, my first attempt at my driving meeting was unsuccessful. I went through the feelings that at the time could only be described as devastating. This occurred long before I discovered the importance of a better mindset; I did receive support from family and friends. This is important, but it's more important that you can manage your own state no matter what happens around you. As you can appreciate entering a world in which you can control your perceptions, emotions and behaviours is perhaps a lot easier than you may have previously imagined. It will take effort and the investment of your time, but the return will be life changing. If it was easy and required no investment it's unlikely you would feel anything near to the same level of satisfaction you will enjoy when you pass. The techniques are not exclusive for driving, they can and I'm sure will be used in your work life, sports and social life, as well as helping you feel more confident and ready to take on challenges you may have turned down in the past. I appreciate how much more difficult achieving a pass is now than it was thirty years ago. The standard required is certainly much higher now, so it's important to remember that your instructor will only advise you to take your driving meeting when they know you are ready. It may seem obvious but it's an important reminder that you are on the brink of a new life, greater freedom and that so many possibilities await you. You are about to step into a new world so instead of hoping that you can get it all out of the way, enjoy the process. Each lesson you have will build your skills as a driver. Finally, I wish you every success, enjoy your lessons and see each one as a stepping stone full of experience that will be invaluable long after you pass.

Drive safely.

Simon.

Copyright. Simon Capon
(October 9th 2020)

All rights reserved. No part of this publication may be reproduced, stored in a retrieval system, or transmitted in any form or by any means, electronically, mechanically, photocopying or recording or otherwise, without the prior written permission of the publisher.

Continued work program.

If you have enjoyed this book and want to further your development regarding any challenges that you face, I run a number of coaching programs. The World is changing fast and we must update our mindset to stay ahead. I've designed and developed a series of coaching programs that equip anyone with the psychological tools required when facing work and personal stress. The programs are face to face meetings, live video, training incognito and long term coaching.

Face to face meetings:

If you are based on the Isle of Wight we can meet for a face to face coaching session at a location that is desirable for you.

Live video coaching:

The majority of my clients live either mainland UK or overseas. I use zoom, WhatsApp or messenger video. Live video training is the same content and quality as the face to face meetings.

Training incognito:

I've been incredible fortunate to work with some amazing individuals and teams over the past fifteen years, but I'm also conscious that there are countless numbers of people who need and want help, but a face to face or video call is a concept they are not comfortable with, or they may wish to remain anonymous. I was relentless in my pursuit for an answer so I designed and developed training incognito. Instead of face to face or phone conversation we simply converse through text and email. The client explains their current difficulties and I write and record a personalised video coaching session.

Long term coaching:

We are living in a fast-changing world. Having a comprehensive psychological toolkit will be a significant advantage for anyone. Mastering the skills that provide solutions for the challenges of today and in the future will place you in a position few will ever experience. Long term coaching is a comprehensive program that unfolds over a period of five months and is totally life changing.

For further details take a look on my website.

www.mindsettrainingisleofwight.com

info@simoncapon.co.uk

Thank you

Simon Capon

Printed in Great Britain
by Amazon